Cats

and

Dogs

Cats

and

Dogs

Scrambler Books
Sacramento, California

Cats and Dogs
©2014 Andrew James Weatherhead
First edition

Published by Scrambler Books
Sacramento, California
www.scramblerbooks.com
Poetry Series no. 13

Cover art collage by Andrew James Weatherhead
Cover design by Jeremy Spencer
This book uses the Perpetua typeface
designed in 1929 by Eric Gill.

ISBN 978-0-578-14588-4
Printed in the United States of America

a medical student in London, for whose knowledge in his profession I have reason to feel great respect, assured me, the other day, that a patient, in recovering from an illness, had got drunk on a beef steak

-Thomas De Quincey

Something That Happened in Brooklyn

This line describes something that happened in Brooklyn.
This line introduces a "you" character
and this line introduces the speaker's relationship to the
    "you" character,
which is vague – yet undoubtedly romantic in nature.

This line describes the weather in Manhattan
and what it looks like from Brooklyn. This line
describes what the "you" is wearing
and this line is possibly metaphorical.

In this line, the speaker remembers walking
with the "you" down a street in Brooklyn.
This line describes how the weather has
changed and how walking is no longer pleasant.

This line describes an apartment
though it's unclear whether it belongs to
the "you" or to the speaker, or whether that matters.
This line describes food or eating in some way.

This line describes the weather again
with an emphasis on the temperature,
which is possibly metaphorical. The final line
describes the tactile quality of a pillow
and uses the adverb "softly."

Brisk October Poem

Clouds gather concentrically overhead.

The weird, creepy church looms large in the distance.

Unfortunately, a poem does not reveal itself.

I continue walking, gathering speed.

The world is in the exact shape of my eyes and I have no
choice but to believe it.

I cross the street and behold a black Range Rover bearing
down on me.

I observe its perfect symmetry slowing down, looking
annoyed.

Briefly, I contemplate a bagel.

Somewhere, someplace it is raining but not that hard.

The phone doesn't ring before you answer it.

Your voice emerges from the darkness like a crystalline
thing.

I forgot what I was going to say so that is what I say.

The things I say are in the exact shape of an email I will send
later.

I think about basketball for the rest of the day.

I see the Golden State Warriors in everything.

St. Patrick's Day

Manual fixation

        isn't really a thing

               but I have it

I think

      this poem would be better

             written in crayon

There's something sloppy

         in the way

                you present yourself

in the way

      your little sister

           got shiny and fat.

The Truth

Outside, a piece of pizza is being rained on –
    the water fills the crust soggy,
    the toppings washed away

From a distance, it looks like my friend Phillip –
    the cheese running down his face,
    the water filling his lungs

Poem

felt your love
like a small poltergeist
of baby fat
in my ear
because I told you
I gave you directions
to follow
and you did
now there's a book about it
you wrote it
haha
haha

Document #5

Document #5 had black and white stripes

It was next to Document #2

The others were lost or had never existed

The black and white stripes looked like an old fashioned
    bottle of coke, the glass kind

And this looked like a bear standing up, which I took as an
    example of intelligent design even though I knew I was
    using the term incorrectly

Document #5 took up the entire screen

I put my name on it and deleted a few things

And slid over to the inkjet printer

I was still learning how to read

The Bag Plopped into the Middle

The bag plopped into the middle

No one saw from where or what it was – if it was a bag even

They just assumed since it held stuff it was

Someone bent down to touch it and someone said it was
    theirs

And between the two of them they argued

It had a mountain on it, the bag did – though it was hard to
    make out because it was moving very fast

In my eyes the trees were a dead giveaway

The tree line too – it was a tall mountain

And seemed very sad

Haiku in the Modern Manner

How tall are you?

I'm not tall.

Haiku in the Traditional Manner

I tried being nice.

It worked.

Non-Fictions

1.
one of my
poems has
a penis in it
and it wets
the bed yes
it's me at the
center of all
this beauty

2.
we talked about
sleds sledding
on other sleds
thank you for
that you small
town girl

3.
all you need to
know is Mick
a 400lbs
woman stuck
in the bathroom
is listening to
everything you
say

4.
raking the leaves
a regatta of
many colored
sails drinking
pink lemonade
we're talking about
me now drifting
in and out of
consciousness

5.
Thornton and
whatever his
name was
holstered their
pistols —
everybody must
get stoned

6.
city of circling
of overlapping circles
someone stomps
his face out with
a golf shoe I
sing top 40
from his bicycle

7.
a few weeks ago
walking into a
corner store I
punched the
well-wisher
Keisha

8.
I stood in front
of a painting
too long I thought
maybe people
change I imagined
Chloë without
her umlaut

9.
eager as ever
I cash my birthday
check I am
only asking
to be remembered

10.
it wasn't easy
rotting away
in prison with
no hands

11.
the FBI
ratted out everyone
they knew

nobody knew
what they
were talking
about

Playing Tennis Against a Wall

The only way to win
is to rent a bulldozer
file a construction permit
learn how to operate
a bulldozer.
Don't be a sore loser.
Trace the thought
back to the beginning.
The bus is late, again
but it's here. It's just you
and the driver.
His ringtone is that
Ennio Morricone song.
You know the one.
He has to use his hands.
He says, "Who is this?"
Then, "Oh, good morning."

Love Poem

Sitting on the roof
I'm not thinking about
other roofs I haven't
sat on. I'm drinking bourbon
from a mug. A man twirls
fire in the distance.
Oh look, there's
two of them.

Friday

first grey
hair arrived
in the library
all day
and all night
nothing to do
but touch it

America

American flag
toothpicks pierce
my sandwich

next to a pickle
I didn't ask for

A Private View of Butt City

From the third floor window
across the blackened sky
a string of lights flickering
on the horizon.
No wait.
Let me start again.
The name of this poem is
"A Private View of Butt City"
and the lights on the horizon
are Butt City. I want to be 100% clear
about this. The lights themselves
are not Butt City, but simply
a Butt City, any Butt City,
not necessarily the genuine
article. And the horizon itself
is not Butt City but
the location of Butt City,
a place where Butt City is located.
And between me and Butt City
there is nothing – no lights
and no horizon – which is scary
though I know somewhere, out there
the wind must be blowing,
which is a kind of something
even if it can't be held or squeezed.
What's arresting though (beyond the lack) is that
Butt City from this vantage
exists in one plane and one
plane only, nothing in front of or
behind the illumined horizon
lying flat like a photograph not yet
crumpled: Butt City from
the guest bedroom in the
cold part of the year.

Thank You Notes

1.
The man at the artist's colony
was only four feet tall.

His face resembled a
peach, a peach blossom,
a rose petal crushed by rain.

The wind's hyacinth motioned
to him. It wanted water.
It was experiencing dehydration.
It needed music.

2.
The man on the elliptical
could fit an elliptical only
in his tiny basement
gymnasium.

He was silent as he moved
and worked up a kind of sweat,
a musk.

After that, he ate his chicken dinner
alone watching *The Sopranos*.
We called him Rose.

3.
A man on the campground
holds me hostage and it's
not racist or anything
when he calls me Pedro.

The cave-like dwelling
in which we were dwelling
made no sense to me even
when mapped.

A gentle wind crushing
my spirits emanated
always.

4.
The man called the President
promised me iced coffee
and you know what?
He delivered.

He looked busy and I said,
"You, don't worry about me."
To which he replied, "The
reason I can't sleep at night
is you" — then he left.

You may recognize yourself
or someone like you in a mirror
or in a window if it's dark outside.

You may also use
the FAFSA to apply
for aid from other sources
such as your state or school.

Love,

The U.S. Department of Education

Haiku after Ishiguro

Years passed.
(He shot a tiger
in the face.)

Poem

You don't even know
you know even half
the stuff you know.
No one is home.
In 2012, 141 people
were killed by trains.

Poems for the Morning Commute

I

alone at the bus
stop this morning
the wind blows but
not hard enough
to move anything
I hear it coming
before it comes
a small bee interrupts
my reading, tries
to pollinate my
sweatshirt
I move away
and return
to find the word
pulchritude
ill-defined by its
context, I read it
twice and forget
the bus arrives

II

a small child confused
by leaves in a trash can
says what I'm thinking

she says *look*

III

are the seats blue for a reason?

in the event of an emergency
will there be an emergency?

like a tongue, the wheelchair ramp does
not reach the ground

Hamilton Avenue turns yellow, then red

is this the woman
with the enormous ear,
the tumor like an earring?

and who says the hunchback
isn't canny, curled up
like a question?

IV

saw
a cat stuck
in a tree

a plastic bag
floating

up to meet it

V

the church light flickers
next to where I wait

matte puddles evaporate
after morning rain

I watch a lone team field
grounders in
a baseless park

they punch the gloved hand
with the ungloved fist

hours later, it's clear
the fog rolled on
the sky a hyperlink blue

the sun making the
windows wince, everything
shot through

VI

scrap metal seen
up close: they spray
water on it
for some reason,
a fine mist it
casts on the windows
as we roll past
a black dog wades
through blue trash
he takes his time
though the days
are getting shorter
the man they call Shakespeare
throws knives
and plays the harmonica
a screenless television
has been here for weeks
now it's home

VII

I press the button
but the button doesn't work

I pull the cord

I write *the way of all meat*

some fat behind the neck

I think, *it's cold*

it's Thursday, I think

I'm cold

VIII

white noise:
clouds

      *

a bus at night:
distrust and light

      *

45° in September:

lilacs in italics

IX

tan and beige park
ranger green with

small brown accolades
pinned to short

sleeves, instead of
a gun she carries

a flashlight feminine
and tough

I feel attracted
to her

and her
presence here, she orders

a cinnamon-
raisin bagel

with pink lox spread
and patrols

that perimeter

X

double parked

leaves

a parking ticket

orange

XI

two buses today: one
and then another
I chose the latter, the later
with fewer people, more seats
and restless drumming
from some young headphones
keeping time

things seen:

        a pale horse
on a black sock

a dog eating hashbrowns

an airplane's shadow

the deciduous sweetgum

a spooky stillness, unimaginable
wealth

XII

a large fly buzzes,
rides for free

*

al-
   monds:

al-
   most a meal

*

the Aerosmith song
I try to forget

XIII

No one knows when the bus will arrive, not even
the computer system tasked with its whereabouts.
Some passengers take this better than others.
One man in grey sweatpants eats a bag of Cheetos
by drinking it; another, half-beautiful woman
voices her complaints to no one.
Sometimes the bus swoops in, scattering papers
and sometimes it stops short – but what I love most
is how the bus always kneels.

XIV

skittle and
lopsided grape

clawed lottery
ticket and grape

two empty
milkshakes

themselves circle

on the
spectacular
floor

XV

a condemned building
advertises its fate
a vacant lot
advertises its fate
the city advertises
its bilingual lawyers
on a placard way above me
the curb rises up
and overtakes my view
we enter a short tunnel
the rain pauses
we exit, lean
around a traffic
circle and
stop

3:21am

a dog barks urgently
at a cat? the moon
shines brightly
despite the clouds.

no cars. the sound
of an ocean-going vessel
maybe.

it's 3:21am on Monday,
I mean Tuesday. each drop
of dew matriculating
in the yard, a reminder
of something left undone.

tomorrow, which today
it is, arrives a little later
than yesterday —
the autumnal burden
of morning relaxed
pushed back
again

CVS

like Target, only smaller
no furniture
same color red
used to be a shoe store
three or four years ago
here on 8th street
the cashier points me
to an automated cashier
machine, but still does
everything for me
cash back means
I don't have to go
to Chase Bank later
I hate Chase Bank

The Cat Gets Bold

the cat
gets bold
it paws
my leg
scratching
my shin
I kick it
and am
looked at
by strangers
but they do
nothing
they do not
know me
they do
not know
this cat
they do
not know
I know
this cat

New Pants

Two years pass in an hour.
The wrong war ends.
I made it to page 257
before the library asked for it back.
Like initials carved into a sapling
that brown and grow apart
as they age, I was ready to
die. I lay down on the floor.
I wanted to look up at the moon
one last time, but forgot which
room I was in. A tiny rift
under the window
let the wind in: it whistled
along the wainscoting.

Poem on the R Train

two brown rivers
of coffee

cross and
come back

they make a lake
of it
by the door

which closes
without warning

turning slightly then
it fans out
in further
proscriptive
rivulets

      until
the source rolls
elsewhere, empty
and dun

End of Summer

even the dogs
don't like it

nothing new
and not getting old

like Han Shan
without a still mind

I watch leaves fall
in a dusty park

earlier I was sure
I wanted a pretzel

but now I know
I'd like a swift death

and no landlord
is a good landlord

so, like
a bad method actor

I packed my things
and left

Poem Above Clouds

in the sky
the cabin writhed
all around me

ensconced in headphones
the unknown
was beyond that

with clouds like funny icebergs
and iceberg lettuce neatly
folded and tucked away

the horizon graded
blue, tan and orange
in that order
      a square sky
over dull peaks

      as we tilt
politely to the right
then harder to the left

and the worst of course
is not the infant crying
but the obese woman
who thinks the baby is hers

her restless soliloquy
conveys what the words
might not:
      she knows
exactly how alone
she is

Take it Easy

the wind blew in
off the lake today
I lifted heavy weights
in the morning with
the help of coffee
I dribbled a basketball
in place I read
about a tiny island
both Korea and Japan
think is theirs I
found a small pimple
in my beard next
to a single red
hair

sitting in the yard, everything is a distraction

where the house and the garage limit
my field of view to a small patch
of sky, the wind picks up and dies

I always forget how tall the trees are
I feel chemicals in me rise while others decline
I think about Shelly dying in that lake

the neighbor's two kids, the two
neighborhood kids, the two kids
who like hockey play soccer

a squirrel shoots sideways along a fence
the barbeque casts a small, severe shadow
the weather whispers what it wants
and we're all powerless against it

I think about my friend
making phone calls in New York
she is and has always been

like the blue bird
sitting in the branch above me
threatening to shit in my hair

her poems are what she says naturally
unaware and in spite of me
that is why I'll love her

Selling Drugs

Sending an email in
2002, you were never sure.
Waking up to is that
a knife in your pocket?
On my hands, in yours
acting like I wanted to.
Making people cry, eating
Oreos, playing basketball
for hours. Any less'd
be too much.

Poem for my neighbor's bird, which I took care of for 10 days while they were in Turkey

Bianca —
diamond-tailed something
I have fed you food
meant for canaries
and finches, of which
you are neither

you ate all of
the seeds and all
but one of the types
of grains and then
I gave you some "grit"
for your digestion

it's not clear
to me how you
eat because you only
seem to smack the dish
with your beak, scattering
food everywhere, and
plus I've never seen
you swallow

at home
I typed "diamond-tailed"
into google and
autocomplete said
you are a dove

so, you are a dove

I see there are
lots of you in Australia

and sometimes you
eat ants

our final afternoon
together you coo'd
at me and pecked
my hand, which drew
blood, then you laid
an egg, which was weird

A Letter

My friend's dad says he's writing a novel based
on a premise he attributes to Samuel Morse that
sound waves never truly die, they just get so small
in amplitude we can't hear them anymore, though
if only we had some way to hone in and amplify them
then we'd have access to all sorts of treasures.

It's not a bad idea actually, and he's encouraged
me to help write it if I want to but leaving his
house tonight I was too full of a weird sadness.
I had recommended we get high and watch
Weekend at Bernie's but it was a big letdown —
neither of us could pay attention and the DVD
skipped over much of the middle third so when
the movie ended and the credits rolled they still
hadn't gone water skiing and my friend's dad
wouldn't believe rigor mortis hadn't played some part.

So I decided to take a lengthy detour by the dark
and windy beach — there's a tree there called Dr. Love
and, legend has it, if you ingest a special fungus
at the right time of day, when the trees turn black
against the purple night, she'll reveal all her
secrets to you.

        Well, I'm writing to you now to say
that yes, I did partake of the special fungus, and yes,
Dr. Love did reveal her secrets to me, but
what I really began to notice that night
were the countless other trees with
even tinier names: oak, elm, & ash

House Fire

I carried the ride cymbal to the neighbor's house
like a giant glass of wine only I know how to drink.

I offered lessons but was rebuffed.
I walked back across the yard trembling.

Then storm clouds stole the day. My stomach hurt.
The skies bled. The passage of time wrapped me up

and delivered me into winter. The ambulance driver
was reading *Harmonium* and crying. All his friends had died in
    a fire, he said.

They probably shouldn't have died in that fire, he said.

Hell Has Gradations

after Max Jacob

My mom walks in.
She asks me how
my writing is going.
"Good," I say. (I'm
lying.) I look up.
The ceiling fan is
shaking a little bit.
There's a stain in
the shape of a fist.
"It's cold in here,"
she says. "I know,"
I say. I'm wearing
sweatpants. She turns
the fan off. "Ok," she
says, "I'm going to
bed." She's wearing
her robe. It's green.
It used to be greener.
She shuffles down
the hall. I stand up.
Even without shoes on
I'm taller than she is
(though she was taller
than me for more years
than I've been taller
than her, so there's
that). A dog barks.
It reminds me of
mine who we had
put down in May.
I commit to writing
something real. *I am
taller than my mom.*

Alex is taller than
my mom. I am taller
than Alex and Griff.
John is taller than me.
Pat is taller than John
and Brett is tallest
of my close friends.
None of them
can save me.

9/9/11

on Sunday, September 11th
turns 10 on the radio
they're talking to people
they talked to ten years ago
one guy I like is this calm
and important lawyer
who, ten years ago,
preached measured action
and adherence, above all,
to the constitution "law
enforcement," he said,
"not assassination" but
nobody listened to him
they accused him of not
being patriotic enough,
of being "soft" on "terror"
for acting so reasonably
after a tragedy, but what
they didn't realize is maybe
reasonable is some people's
steady state, like when they
aren't anything else they are
just sort of numb and reasonable
they don't try to undo what
can't be undone, they don't
point fingers or get drunk any more
than they have to, they just like
reading books and bowling
with their friends, and might
even be found singing karaoke
to a roomful of strangers

Washington, George

anger of appeal of architecture and
landscape design to appointment as
commander-in-chief armed schooners
sent to prey on enemy shipping by
assassination plot against birth of
British acquisition of secret letters by
burning of New York considered by
character and personality of church attendance
of councils of war called by criticism of daily
review of troops and defenses by decision to make
a stand in New York by diaries of discipline
and leadership of dislike of New Englanders by
early military career of enlistment of free blacks
authorized by fortifications ordered built by
honors and tributes accorded to horsemanship of
impeccable uniform and grooming of imposing
physical appearance and stature of intelligence
gathered by lifestyle and hospitality of
maps and drawings available to marriage
and family life of military "family" in residence
with military indecisiveness and mistakes of
New York country residences of New York
retreat planned and carried out by
payment for service rejected by periods
of discouragement and distress of
perseverance and determination of personal
and domestic staff of personal instructions
to the army by plantation home of (see
Mount Vernon) political judgment of
portrait of realism of respect of officers and
men for rudimentary education of
self-command and precision of slaves
owned by smallpox attack of
splitting up the army by

strategic military planning of
surveying work of
Virginia legislative
service of wealth and
social position of

Me, You, and Everyone We Knew

we talked about shopping online: the items
we would and would not feel comfortable doing
that with; I said, "shoes," you agreed

I liked the iced tea, you didn't
you drank the orange juice
you looked around the room

we both looked around the room
the Isotopes, you reminded yourself, was
a reference to *The Simpsons*, the baseball team

and it had been revealed recently that Springfield
was in Oregon, a map of which
happened to be on the wall

a whole lot of people got up and left
we talked about the heat, the day, our friend Brett;
we talked about our age, the town we now

felt unwelcome in, the weekend;
you were moving away, slowly, and I was moving
away even slower, though had further to go

regarding the hash browns, we both felt underserved;
we talked more about museums, those drone things,
the war, and then it was afternoon and time to go

your girlfriend pulled up in a white jeep
and a green shirt and claimed you had
somewhere more important to be

What Happens When Your Dad Dies

what happens when your dad dies

is you get a phone call

is he going to be ok, you ask

you hear "no" and crying

you don't say anything

for so long that someone says

"are you still there?"

you say "yeah"

the phone gets passed around

someone says you have a flight home

someone says to book a car, use the credit card

someone says to not forget your suit

the call ends

you sit down

you stand

you email your boss and roommates

you take a long shower

and walk outside

it's 3:13 in the morning

a garbage truck is beeping

you start walking

you take a left, a right, another left

then walk straight for a while

you come to a brightly lit diner

you open the door

it's empty except for the wait staff

you sit in a booth

you order the steak and eggs

no meal in your entire life

has arrived so crystal clear

and meaningless

there're onions and green peppers

in the hash browns

a very small glass of juice

you manage a few bites

ESPN is on the television

the NBA playoffs

are about to begin

and months later you'll realize

you just got up and left

completely forgetting to pay

and that sucks

because they

were really nice

Acknowledgements

The author would like to thank the editors of the following journals in which some of these poems originally appeared: *juked*, *The Scrambler*, *Her Royal Majesty*, *The Broome Street Review*, *Metazen*, *Keep This Bag Away From Children*, *Pop Serial*, *Midnite Snak*, *Aesthetix*, *Banango Street*, *Shallow*, *West 10th*, *Augury Books*, *3:AM Magazine*, *Entertainment Weekly*, *Everyday Genius*, *Monster House Press*, *So and So Magazine* and *Painted Bride Quarterly*.

About the Author

Andrew James Weatherhead holds a degree in Neuroscience from NYU, an MFA in Creative Writing from The New School, and is an Eagle Scout. He lives in Brooklyn, New York, where he walks dogs. This is his first book.

www.scramblerbooks.com